THIS WALKER BOOK BELONGS TO:

_____

_____

_____

_____

The bats are thirsty,
Starved and thin;
The moon is full,
So COME ON IN!

For Françoise

First published 1990 by
Walker Books Ltd
87 Vauxhall Walk, London SE11 5HJ

This edition published 2000

Text and illustrations © 1990 Colin McNaughton

This book has been typeset in Caslon 540.

Printed in Hong Kong

British Library Cataloguing in Publication Data
A catalogue record for this book is
available from the British Library.

ISBN 0-7445-7535-4 (hb)
ISBN 0-7445-7779-9 (pb)

WHO'S BEEN SLEEPING IN MY PORRIDGE?

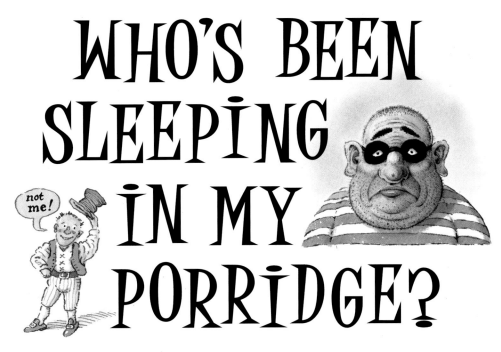

A Book of Wacky Poems and Pictures

Colin McNaughton

WALKER BOOKS

AND SUBSIDIARIES

LONDON • BOSTON • SYDNEY

He's called Dennis, Miss.

THE LION'S DEN

"Bring all your pets in tomorrow,
We'll all have a jolly nice time."
To teacher, a pet means a gerbil;
She obviously hasn't seen mine!

SMEDLEY WAS DEADLY

Smedley was deadly,
    A spitter supreme;
He spat through his teeth
    In short bursts or a stream.
He spat with such force,
    Yet with wonderful style;
Our mothers thought
    Smedley was perfectly vile!
Yes, Smedley was boring
    And hardly a wit –
But Smedley was special
    'cause boy could he spit!

HAPPY HARRY

Happy Harry
Laughed all day,
Couldn't keep
A smile away.

But one sad day –
A tragedy:
A car hit Harry,
Fatally.

Poor old Harry.
Beep-beep-honk!
Laughed his head off –
Ha, ha, bonk!

GOOD ENOUGH TO EAT

Oh, what a cute puppy, look, do.
Oh do come and see – coochee-coo!
He's such a sweet pup,
I could eat him right up –
We'll have him tonight in a stew!

A GIANT GORILLA ONCE CAME UP TO ME

(An extract from the autobiography of ffotherington-
   ffortesque-fforbes-ffarquhar.)

A giant gorilla once came up to me
   And started to push me around.
I put up me dukes, gave him one of me looks
   And set about holding me ground.

I'm ffotherington-ffortesque-fforbes-ffarquhar
   (Forty-seventh in line to the throne);
For a ffotherington-ffortesque-fforbes-ffarquhar
   To retreat, has never been known!

But this bounder had obviously not read *Debrett's*:
   He responded by beating his chest.
So I leaped via his knee up into a tree
   And stunned him with six of the best!

Take that Sir and that Sir and that Sir and that!
   (I enjoy nothing more than a scrap.)
With a howl and a squeal, he then turned on his heel;
   "That'll teach you to bully a chap!"

Yes, I'm ffotherington-ffortesque-fforbes-ffarquhar
   (Forty-seventh in line to the throne);
For a ffotherington-ffortesque-fforbes-ffarquhar
   To retreat, has never been known.

ITCHY FEET

A man went out and bought a car.

But the poor man's car didn't go very far.

    (The wheels fell off!)

So the man went out and bought another,

But this turned out just like the other.

    (It had no engine!)

So the man went out and bought a third,

A fifty-seven Thunderbird!

White-wall tyres, chopped real low,

One small problem: wouldn't go.

    (Big end gone!)

So he changed his tack and bought a ship,

But the ship sprung a leak on its very first trip.

    (Man the lifeboats!)

So the man went out and bought a plane,

But the poor man had no luck again.

    (It flew south for the winter!)

So the man went out and bought a horse,
And the horse went very well, of course.
But the trouble was – it wouldn't stop.
Cheerio horsy, clop-clip, clop-clip, clop. . .

So the man went out and bought a balloon,
But the hot-air balloon went off too soon.
    (He hadn't tied the basket on!)

So the man went out and bought a crow,
But that big black crow didn't want to know.
    (Who can blame him?)

So the man went out and bought a duck,
But once again he was out of luck.
    (The duck was quackers!)

So the man went out and bought a flea,
Which might seem silly to you or me,
But not as mad as it first sounds –
He can travel the world in leaps and bounds.

    (A Hoppy Ending.)

DEAD FUNNY

Robot's dead,
Lack of grease.
Parson said:
"Rust in peace."

MY BEST FRIEND BOB

My best friend Bob
Has a terrible job
With his dad, who's definitely dippy.
    He sits in his chair,
      With flowers in his hair
And his headphones on – he's a hippy!

JACK THE LAD

"Will you boys stop those fisticuffs!
    Who started all this, Jack?"

"The truth is, Sir, it all began
    When Henry hit me back!"

IF I WAS A BIRD

If I was a bird,
My wings I would spread,
I'd swoop over you
And plop on your head!

MUM IS HAVING A BABY!

Mum is having a baby!
I'm shocked! I'm all at sea!
What's she want another one for:
WHAT'S THE MATTER WITH ME!?

IF EVER ALIENS

If ever aliens should visit the earth,
With googly eyes and skin bright green,
And they come down to London
To visit the Queen,
We'll have one thing in common,
It's an absolute cert:
It won't be our hairstyles,
Or the cut of our shirt,
Or relations in Eastbourne,
Or choice of dessert.

It'll be that our babies,
Though black, green or pink,
Have one thing in common:
They, all of them, STINK!

BOXING DAY

If ever my mum and my dad had a fight,
There's no doubt in my mind at all;
    Mum would annihilate father because,
She's huge and he's terribly small!

WHO'S BEEN SLEEPING IN MY PORRIDGE?

"Who's been sitting in my bed?"
   said the mummy bear crossly.
"Who's been eating my chair?"
   said the baby bear weepily.
"Who's been sleeping in my porridge?"
   said the papa bear angrily.
"Wait a minute," said Goldilocks.

"Why can't you guys just stick
   to the script? Now let's try
   it again and this time no messing about."

ON YOUR HEAD BE IT!

If you're poor and in distress,
Without a bean and penniless,
Your head is cold, your bonce is blue,
Then this is my headvice to you:
Wear a teapot, wear a shoe,
Lift it up, say "How de do!"
Wear a sock, wear a pan,
Wear a king-size baked-bean can.
Wear a saucer, wear a cup,
Wear a plantpot, downside up.
Wear a bucket, wear a bowl,
Wear the tube from a toilet roll.
Wear a lampshade, wear a vase,
Wear a fishbowl, man from Mars!

Wear a pie (not too hot!),
Wear a sooty chimneypot.
Wear a matchbox, wear a book,
For that literary look.
Wear an eggcup, plain or spotty,
Wear a washed-out baby's potty.
Wear a yellow traffic cone,
Wear a big brass bass trombone.
Wear an orange rubber glove,
Wear a housetrained turtle-dove.
Wear a ball, a loaf of bread,
A ripe banana – use your head!

Your head's in the sand if you can't see it.
If you catch cold, ON YOUR HEAD BE IT!

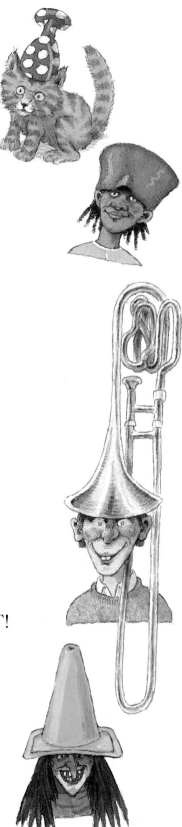

GIANTS I HAVE KNOWN

Of all the giants I have met,
Here are a few I can't forget:
Giant Grim was tall and slim,
While Giant Splatt was round and fat.
Giant Grave was strong and brave,
While Giant Howard was a downright coward.
Giant Grart was always smart,
While Giant Tess was a proper mess.
Giant Shnean was cruel and mean,
While Giant Tweet was soft and sweet.
Giant Floon was bald as a spoon,
While Giant Camilla looked like a gorilla.
Giant McGrew was honest and true,
While Giant Mulroney, appeared to me phony.
Giant Delaney was ever so brainy,
While Giant Shabim was incredibly dim.
Giant Skewark could sing like a lark,
While Giant Von Krup got told to shut up.
Giant O'Gloot had tootsies minute,
While Giant O'Groats had feet like rowboats.
But the strangest giant I've met in my time,
If I brought all the others and stood them in line,
He'd stand out a mile and you'd see what I mean –
He's the weirdest giant that I've ever seen.
He's charming, polite and his first name is Ken,
He weighs seven stone and he stands – four foot ten!

Good day!

THE BALLAD OF FIRTILSTERN UNITED

The strangest game I've ever seen,
Was a crazy football match between
The Himalayan Mountain team
And Firtilstern United.

The pitch sloped eighty-five degrees,
It wasn't grass, but rocks and trees,
And the referee ignored the pleas
Of Firtilstern United.

The home team seemed equipped to cope,
With climbing boots and climbing rope;
There really wasn't any hope
For Firtilstern United.

The referee in overcoat,
Was a Himalayan mountain goat;
And victory seemed quite remote
For Firtilstern United.

Half-time came and went, no score,
Ice picks issued, furthermore,
The game had much worse things in store
For Firtilstern United.

One by one their players fell,
The subs came on and fell as well;
As the last man went, we said farewell
To Firtilstern United.

But as he fell, heroic soul,
With quite uncommon ball control,
He looped the loop and scored a goal
For Firtilstern United.

And as the final whistle blew,
The home team knew what they must do:
Salute the Captain and the crew
Of Firtilstern United.

The Himalayan Mountaineers,
Despite their first defeat in years,
Gentlemanly gave three cheers
For Firtilstern United.

But as they clapped their hands, oh woe,
Let go their ropes and fell, oh no!
They landed with a squelch below
On Firtilstern United.

MRS MATHER

Scared stiff.
Courage flown.
On that doorstep all alone.
Cold sweat.
State of shock.
Lift my trembling hand and knock.

Thumping heart.
Chilled with fear.
I hear the witch's feet draw near.
Rasping bolts.
Rusty locks.
Shake down to my cotton socks.

Hinges creaking.
Waft of mould.
A groan that makes my blood run cold.
Cracking voice.
Knocking knees.
"Can I have my ball back, please?"

READ ALL ABOUT IT!

EXTRA! EXTRA!

"Extra! Extra! Read all about it!
Two men swindled! The latest news!"

"You there! Newsboy! Sell me a paper,
That's an offer I can't refuse. . .!
Hey, there's nothing about a swindle!
Not one word or a why, where, whose!"

"Extra! Extra! Read all about it!
Three men swindled! The latest news!"

OVERHEARD AT THE T. REX TAVERNA

"Gimme a roast Pterodactyl
with a side order of Mammoth
followed by a pickled Stegosaurus.
(Hold the horns!)
Then I think I'll have the
Bronto-burger with french fries!"

"And for dessert, Sir?"

"Let me see. Yep, a baked Diplodocus
with maple syrup.
Oh yeah, an' a cup of coffee –
but no sugar – got to watch
the old waistline, you know!"

TODAY'S
MENU
TRICERATOPS
CHOPS
COELACANTH
and CHIPS
ARCHAEOPTERYx
a l'ORANGE
BRONTO BURGERS

BONES
BUCKET

THE MOON IS FULL

The moon is full, you can't get moved.
I'm not going back till it's improved!
It's fit to burst, it's overrun
With aliens in search of fun.

Every crater's jam-packed full;
They say low gravity's the pull.
Those package tours that come from Earth
Make sure they get their money's worth.

Silly T-shirts, solar flares,
Tinted helmets, no one cares!
Hotels as far as the eye can see
Surround the Sea of Tranquillity.

There's no room to swing a cat,
Just souvenirs and tourist tat.
Smaller craters (there are no rules!)
Converted into swimming pools!

I want to know, when on vacation,
What is people's motivation?
It baffles me why every race
Should crowd together in one place.

You'd think they'd search for peace and quiet.
It beats me why they never try it.
Alien life forms, cheek by jowl,
The smell of suntan oil is foul!

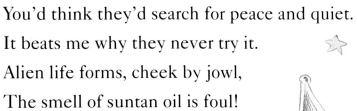

Fun-fairs, drive-ins, fast-food bars,
The stink of duty free cigars.
I used to come for a month in June,
But that was before the tourist boom.

Next vacation I'll steer clear –
The moon has lost its atmosphere!

THEY CALL ME HARLEY. MAN, AH'M COOL!

They call me Harley.
Man, Ah'm cool!
Ah'm jest a
Motorcyclin' fool.

Ah'm eight years old,
An'tough as boots,
Ah like studs
An' leather suits.

Ah'm so hot
Ah almos' boil!
Ah grease mah hair
With engine oil!

In life the three things
That Ah need:
Mah bike, the open road,
And speed!

Outa mah way!
Here Ah come.
Hear mah engine
Brum brum brum!

Hit the road,
An' hit the gas,
See me comin',
Let me pass!

Mum's a biker,
Dad's one too.
So what's a kid
Supposed to do?

To motorcyclin'
Ah was drawn –
A biker isn't made –
He's born!

FLINCH!

There's a game for two
We play at school,
It's easy as pie,
Only got one rule.
Anyone can play,
It's really a cinch:
The game is simply known as "Flinch".

Two people stand
And face each other,
A yard apart,
And stare at one another.
One throws a punch,
But pulls up short,
The other stands still
Or they might get caught!

If you move your face
Just a smidgin of an inch,
The puncher beats the punchee
And he must shout – FLINCH!

And that's "Flinch".

TALL STORY

I went to the theatre to cheer myself up,
I was hoping to have a few laughs.
   But I found, don't you know,
   The entire front row,
Had been booked by a bunch of giraffes!

DORIS THE PIRATE

Now I'll tell you the story
Of my dear old mum,
Who's taken to cursing
And drinking of rum.

She carries a cutlass
And flintlocks, a pair.
She shoulders a parrot,
And I wouldn't care

But she goes into Safeways
And just for a laugh,
She rides on the trolleys
And threatens the staff.

"Avast there me hearties,
By the curse o' big Frank!
Hand o'er yer treasure
Or y'll all walk the plank!"

She sails down the aisle,
Sliding past frozen food,
Frightening old ladies,
So you might conclude

That my mum is crazy
And completely daft,
She's gone off her trolley,
She's fell off her raft.

She knocks over piles
Of carefully stacked tins,
Cries, "Shiver me timbers!"
Spits, curses and grins.

With her three-cornered hat
And her peg-leg and patch,
The manager knows
That he is no match

For my pirate mum
As she sails through his store;
He hides in his office
An' double locks his door.

He phones the police,
But they never turn out –
Not when Doris the Pirate
Is out and about!

They just have to wait
Till she's finished her fun,
Then count up the cost
Of the damage she's done.

Then they make out a list
And they send us the bill;
It runs into thousands –
This adds to the thrill!

But Mum isn't bothered,
She just shouts "Har, har!"
Then picks up her shovel
And jumps in the car,

Drives to the airport
And hops on a jet,
Is back the next day
Wi' a curse an' a threat!

She bursts through the door
Wi' a "Ya-har, yo, ho!
I've bin diggin' f' treasure,
Ye might like t' know!"

She dumps down a chest
Full of jewels and gold
That were once the possession
Of pirates of old.

Wi' the freshly dug treasure,
We sort out the trouble,
She pays all her debts –
(In fact they get double!)

Since Mum bought the map
In that shop for a pound,
She now knows where
All sorts of treasure is found.

Yes, my mum's a pirate,
It's changed all our plans,
We live on a galleon
In Lytham St Annes!

It's big and it's wooden,
Weighs six hundred tons,
Has masts an' an anchor
An' ninety-eight guns!

I can't go to school now,
Because, to be frank,
Mum will threaten teachers
With walking the plank!

That plenty of mothers
Have jobs, I've no doubt,
"It's perfectly normal!"
I hear you all shout.

But my mum's a pirate,
Her ways she won't mend,
And sometimes we wonder. . .
Where will it all end?

THAT'S THE WAY TO DO IT!

There was an old woman
    Who lived in a shoe,
She had so many children
    She didn't know what to do;
So she sought the advice
    Of her friend Mr Punch,
Who said fry them with onions
    And eat them for lunch!

THE TRIAL

Ladies and gentlemen –
In court today,
Wearing a red nose
And Frenchman's beret,
A dangerous villain,
To whom you must say:
We accuse you of not growing up!

Accounts of your crimes
Take up page after page,
Always playing the fool,
Never acting your age;
With behaviour like this
You should work on the stage.
We accuse you of not growing up!

We've witnesses lined up,
Respectable men:
Accountants, solicitors,
Vicars, amen;
And their evidence proves it
Again and again –
We accuse you of not growing up!

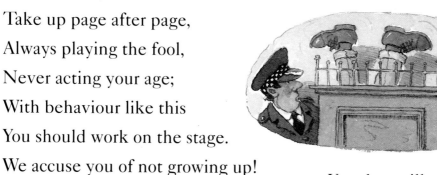

You draw silly pictures
And write silly verse;
We've found them in bookshops,
But really, what's worse,
You should be maturing
But it's the reverse.
We accuse you of not growing up!

You were seen on a skateboard
In Kensington Park,
And shouting at boaters,
"Behind you a shark!"
When asked why you did it
You said "For a lark."
We accuse you of not growing up!

Members of the Jury,
There can be no doubt,
He cannot be serious,
Joking throughout;
When I asked him his job
He said "Messing about!"
We accuse you of not growing up!

Silence in court!
Are the jury agreed?
We've evidence damning,
Much more than we need;
So, Mr McNaughton,
How do you plead?

"Guilty, Your Honour, as charged.
Tra-la. Guilty, Your Honour,
As charged!"

WHY ARE THE KIDS SO MEAN AT SCHOOL?

Why are kids so mean at school?
  Why do they call me the eight-eyed ghoul?
Why are the kids at school so cheeky?
  Why do they call me weird and freaky?

Is it because I'm green and lumpy,
  Could this be why they're all so jumpy?
Or could it be because I'm tall,
  Nine foot six, while they're so small?

Could it be, do you suppose,
  Where they have eyebrows, I have toes?
Where their hair's brown or blond, mine's blue,
  Where they have one head I have two?

Or could it be, can I assume,
  I'm taking up their elbow room?
I may be causing them alarms
  When I put up all seven arms.

You want to hear the way they talks
  About my eyeballs stuck on stalks,
The rude remarks about my smell;
  They laugh at the way I steam, as well!

I know I'm different, well, big deal;
That doesn't mean that I don't feel!
I can't work out the human race –
I'm just a kid from outer space.

NIGHT LIFE

One and two,
Baby done a pooh.
Three and four,
Baby done some more.

Baby start to whimper,
Baby start to cry,
Wakes his mum and daddy up;
Mummy gives a sigh.

"I did it last, Dad,
Your turn now."
Daddy not so sure of this;
"Lazy old cow."

Daddy take the nappy,
Drop it in the bin.
Put another clean one on
And tuck the baby in.

"Nighty-night, baby.
Nighty-night, son."
Baby go to sleep again,
Three, two, one.

Daddy back in bed now,
Mummy gets a cuddle.
Baby is awake again,
Lying in a puddle.

Up you get, Mummy,
Baby done a pee.
No sleep for you tonight,
No siree!

A GOTTLE O' GEAR

"Yes, Sir. What can I get you?"
asked the man behind the bar.

"A gottle o' gear an' a gag o' nuts,"
answered the second-rate ventriloquist
without moving his lips once.

TO BALDLY GO. . .

Where are the forests,
    The deep blue seas?
Where are the mountains,
    The birds and bees?
From space this planet
    Looked so green,
But now I'm here,
    It's pink; I mean
It's pink and smooth,
    Without a feature,
Without a trace
    Of living creature.
I've never seen
    A place so bleak;
But wait a moment –
    As I speak
Something's coming
    After me:
It looks . . . it can't be!
    It's a flea!
It's a monster,
    Big as a house;
I'm being attacked
    By a giant louse!

I'm blasting off,
I'm in the air,
I've almost made it,
Almost there.
But here it comes –
With one last leap,
He's got me!
Crackle . . . zzzt . . . blip . . . bleep. . .

49

MY HERO

And he's coming round the bend at a fantastic speed!

One hundred, two hundred,

Three hundred miles an hour!

He's going past the British champion,

He's going past the American champion,

Now he's in the lead.

Four hundred, five hundred,

Six hundred miles an hour!

How does he keep the machine in control?

The man is fantastic.

A genius.

But wait a minute –

There's still someone ahead of him.

Oh! No!

It's the world champion Wilfred Blackwell!

On his nuclearpowered-turbo-thrust

jet-engined-million-cc-super-bike!

Can McNaughton catch him?

No! It's impossible.

But somehow he's doing it.

And now he's pulling away.

And he's done it!

He's taken the chequered flag.

He's the new champion!

The fastest boy in the history of the world.

My hero.

THE THIRD WORST POME WOT I EVER RITTED

Simple Simon met a pieman
   Going to the fair.
Said Simple Simon to the pieman,
   "Can I have an ice-cream please?"

NOSHER AND ROSIE LAVENDER

Nosher Lavender,
Five years old,
Sweet as sugar,
Good as gold;
Always does
What he is told –
That's lovely Nosher Lavender.

Rosemary Lavender,
Unlike her brother,
Is a thorn in the side
Of her poor mother;
Rosie Lavender's
Like no other –
That's naughty Rosie Lavender.

Rosie breaks things,
Nosher never,
Rosie's dim,
While Nosher's clever;
She fools around,
He, hardly ever –
That's Nosh and Rosie Lavender.

Rosie's noisy,
Nosher's quiet,
Rosie wets it,
Nosher dries it,
Rosie feasts,
Nosher diets –
That's Nosh and Rosie Lavender.

Rosie's brazen,
Nosher's shy,
Nosher's honest,
Rosie's sly;
Say hello,
She'll say goodbye –
That's Nosh and Rosie Lavender.

Who's the cleanest?
Nosher wins;
Funny smells,
Rosie grins;
You'd never guess
That they were twins!
Not Nosh and Rosie Lavender.

BOMB APPETIT!

"If you eat one more slice of pie,
  Then you will burst, I fear."

"Oh, that's a risk I'll gladly take.
  But just in case – stand clear!"

MORE PIE!

FAIR GAME

"Now where have I seen
These tracks before?"
Said the big game hunter fair;
A train came along
And knocked him down,
And then he remembered where!

I RAN AWAY WITH THE CIRCUS

I ran away with the circus,
    Not even stopping to pack.
I ran away with the circus,
    But Mum made me take it back!

SAID THE BOY TO THE DINOSAUR

Said the boy to the dinosaur:
  "Outa my way!"
Said the dinosaur:
  "That's not a nice thing to say."

Said the boy to the dinosaur:
  "Go take a hike!"
Said the dinosaur:
  "Not an expression I like."

Said the boy to the dinosaur:
  "Move aside Mac!"
Said the dinosaur:
  "Obviously, manners you lack."

Said the boy to the dinosaur:
  "Go fly a kite!"
Said the dinosaur:
  "That's what I call impolite."

Said the boy to the dinosaur:
  "Jump in the lake!"
Said the dinosaur:
  "That is as much as I'll take!"

The monster was cross,
  Which is what you'd expect;
"I'm older than you,
  You should show some respect!"

He taught him a lesson,
What more can I say?
The dinosaur ate him
And went on his way.

Outa my way!

QUIFF

Let's celebrate that wonder,
    That overhanging cliff:
The 1950's oiled, spring-loaded
    Rock and roller's quiff!

A marvel of engineering,
    Never seen skew-whiff:
The 1950's oiled, spring-loaded
    Rock and roller's quiff.

NOTHING IS WORSE THAN A FROG IN THE THROAT

The fisherman sang
As he sat in his boat,
A lilting song
Of life afloat.
But he suddenly choked
And he spluttered, I quote:
"Nothing is worse
Than a frog in the throat!"

(It can't be very pleasant for the frog either!)

DAVY DUFF

In our street, Davy Duff
Is king of the castle – mister tough.
   (He's a nanimal!)

He sprayed this message on our wall:
"Davy Duff'll duff you all!"
   (He just doesn't care!)

He's the boss, we're his slaves;
Heard the rumour? Duffy shaves!
   (So Wilfred says!)

Dave's a norphan, doesn't care,
Got no parents, got no hair.
   (He's a loony!)

Dave's a skinhead, only ten;
Goes to school, now and then.
   (When he feels like it.)

Norphan south, east or west,
Dave's the hardest, Dave's the best.
   (It's undisputed!)
He can't read, he can't write,
Davy Duff's not too bright!
   (But don't tell him I said so!)

Well behaved? Davy's not!
We say "Pardon" Dave says "Wot!"
   (He drives our teacher potty.)

Run along and play with your friends, David.

Yus, gran!

Davy Duff lives with his gran;
Davy's gran's his only fan.
   (He's the apple of her eye.)

Davy's gran won't hear a word
Said against him, it's absurd.
   (She says he's misunderstood!)

Davy's gran says it's a sin
That everyone should pick on him.
   (Ha!)
"He's a norphan, got no mam.
Got no dad, poor wee lamb."
   (Poor wee lamb!)

So if you're ever in our street
And Davy Duff by chance should meet . . .
   (Heaven help you!)
Cross the road and don't act tough –
You just can't win with Davy Duff!
   (He's world class!)

Run for it!

DEAD CERTAINTY

I wouldn't be seen dead in a coffin,
I wouldn't be seen dead in a hearse,
I wouldn't be seen dead in a graveyard,
I can't think of anything worse.

POTTY

Don't put that potty on your head, Tim.

Don't put that potty on your head.

   It's not very clean

    And you don't know where it's been,

So don't put that potty on your head.

OH, THE EMBARRASSMENT

Oh, the embarrassment!
　Oh, the disgrace!
I'll never be able to show my face!

I'll never forgive her!
　She said I looked cute!
Mum sent me to school in a sailor suit!

THAT LITTLE MONSTER FRANKENSTEIN

He's really gone too far this time
(The count's son – Master Frankenstein);
He came with Igor late last night
And sneaked around by candlelight.

Those two horrors were apparently seen
Up to snow good on the village green:
Stealing snowmen, bit by bit,
Body snatching – picture it!

A bit from here and a bit from there
Sliced off with a surgeon's care;
Then pulled their cart, with creak and whine
Back to Castle Frankenstein.

Unless their ways those black sheep mend,
Those boys will come to a sticky end,
And we can only contemplate
What monster problems they'll create!

THE CROCODILE'S BRUSHING HIS TEETH

The crocodile's brushing his teeth, I'm afraid,
    This certainly means we're too late.
The crocodile's brushing his teeth, I'm afraid,
    He has definitely put on some weight.
The crocodile's brushing his teeth, I'm afraid,
    It really is, oh, such a bore.
The crocodile's brushing his teeth, I'm afraid,
    He appears to have eaten class four!

THE UN APPY BURGULLER

I'm not an 'appy burguller,
As you can plainly see,
I'm not an 'appy burguller
Cos sum won's burgulled me!

PIG IGNORANT

When I was small, I had a pig.
> *No you didn't!*
>> Yes I did!

He wore a powdered periwig.
> *No he didn't!*
>> Yes he did!

He wore a suit of royal blue silk.
> *No he didn't!*
>> Yes he did!

And dined on plums and buttermilk.
> *No he didn't!*
>> Yes he did!

He slept each night on a featherbed.
> *No he didn't!*
>> Yes he did!

With a fancy hat upon his head.
> *He didn't did he?*
>> Yes he did!

He'd ride a bicycle to town.
> *He didn't did he?*
>> Yes he did!

Just to knock the butcher down.
> *He didn't did he?*
>> Yes he did!

My pig would jump from the roof of his sty.

Did he really?

Yes he did!

Flap his ears and pigs would fly.

Did he really?

Yes he did!

If this is true, this story's big!

Well believe it or not. I don't care a fig!

Not a word of a lie, from the plums to the wig?

Nothing but the truth. (Except the bit about the pig.)

Is it a bird?

Is it a 'plane?

No, it's a pig!

DON'T STICK THAT MARBLE UP YOUR NOSE!

Don't stick that marble up your nostril,
Don't shove that marble up your nose.
    Your mum will have a fit,
     Besides, it's hard to hit!
So don't shove that marble up your nose.

BEWARE THE BEASTLY BOGEYMAN

Beware the beastly bogeyman,
  The googly-eyeballed bogeyman.
Beware the beastly bogeyman,
  He'll have your guts for garters.

I ONCE SAW A FISH UP A TREE

I once saw a fish up a tree,

And this fish he had legs, believe me.

Said the monster, "I'll swear,

I'm just taking the air."

Then he jumped down and ran off to sea.

SOMETIMES I THINK YOU DON'T LISTEN TO A WORD I SAY!

Did you have a hard day at the office, dear?

The usual, you know, nothing special, I fear;
I fell in with pirates and lost both my knees,
Came down with ffotherington's foot-rot disease!
Was mugged by an octopus, chased by a pig,
On the bus a banana set fire to my wig.
I met a magician who sawed me in two
And I had to be stuck back together with glue.
I encountered a cow who was over the moon,
The lift-cable snapped and I plunged to my doom.
I was beaten at chess by a chocolate éclair,
I looked in the mirror, but I wasn't there!
Ran off with the circus, became, if you please,
The daring young man on the flying trapeze.
Had words with an alien, barked at a dog,
Married a dinosaur, fell off a log.
I rescued a man who was falling asleep,
Had lunch with a wood louse (a right little creep!),
Was kidnapped at gunpoint by Princess Diana,
Trussed up in a sack and then dumped in Havana;
Escaped without problem: I hijacked a jet,
Flew home to England and guess who I met?
The Princess and Princes Anne, Charles, Andrew, Eddy. . .

That's very nice dear, your dinner is ready.

Dinner's ready dear.

IF YOU'RE WORRIED 'CAUSE YOU'RE LITTLE

If you're worried 'cause you're little,
  Then I'll tell you what I've found:
The only time to worry's when
  Your feet don't reach the ground!

HERE KITTY, KITTY

"Here Kitty, Kitty,"
Said the man from the city.
The tiger said, "Delighted!"
   The big cat purred
   And said, "My word,
So nice to be invited!"

LAZY MAISY'S OUT OF BED

Lazy Maisy's out of bed,
   Just as day is dawning.
She only does this once a year,
   And that's on Christmas morning.

THE INSULT

(Only read this to someone if [a] they are
much smaller than you or [b] you're an
extremely fast runner!)

Look at that horrible thing on your neck!
It's terrible! Look in the mirror and check.
It's spotty and hairy and ugly and red,
But no need to panic. It's only your head!

IT MUST BE THE DEVIL IN ME

I'd love to write of noble thoughts,
 Of daring deeds and high ideals,
But I write odes to jellied eels!
 It must be the devil in me.

I'd love to write of butterflies,
 Of ladybirds and bumblebees,
But what comes out are slugs and fleas!
 It must be the devil in me.

I'd love to write of twinkling stars,
 And rhyme such words as moon and June,
But I'd make moon rhyme with – spittoon!
 It must be the devil in me.

I'd love to write of daffodils,
 Of fluffy clouds and rosy cheeks,
Believe you me, I've tried for weeks!
 It must be the devil in me.

I'd love to write of nightingales,
 Of turtle doves and meadow larks,
But out come hammerheaded sharks!
 It must be the devil in me.

I'd love to write of maidens fair,
 Of gallantry and heroes bold,
But all that stuff just leaves me cold –
 It must be the devil in me.

I'd love to write of bunnies' tails,
 Of puppy dogs and kittens' paws,
But I just have this thing about dinosaurs!
 It must be the devil in me.

I'd love to write of dark despair
 And misery in ancient Rome,
But I get enough of that at home!
 It must be the devil in me.

I'd love to write of history,
 Of battles won and heroes grim,
But when I try – the baddies win!
 It must be the devil in me.

I'd love to write nice poetry,
 I'd like to be serious once in a while,
But I yam what I yam – I'm juvenile!
 It must be the devil in me.

THE HUMAN BEANPOLE

The thinnest man I ever saw
Was called "the human beanpole".
He'd never open any door,
But slip in through the keyhole!

I'M GARGLING IN THE RAIN

(To the tune of *Singing in the Rain*)

Do be do do, do be, do be do do.
I'm singing in the rain,
   Just singing in the rain,
Gargle glorious feeling,
   Glub glargle again.
Blargle glargle garlgle glog,
Glargle gargle glargle glob,
Blar-blargle, glub gargle in the rain.

THE THREE ERS

Spelling's a doddle,
As easy as pie –
M-I-S-S, I-S-S,
I-P-P . . . er . . .

Arithmetic's kids' stuff,
A piece of cakc, when
Two times four,
Add two, make . . . er . . .

Grammar's a cinch,
It's real easy meat –
The plural of foot
Is obviously . . . er . . .

Please Miss.
That's easy!

WHEN I GROW UP

When I grow up
I would like to be
Rich and famous
On TV.

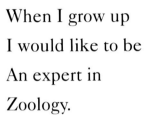

When I grow up
I would like to be
A mermaid
In the deep blue sea.

When I grow up
I would like to be
A baker in a
Bakery.

When I grow up
I would like to be
An expert in
Zoology.

When I grow up
I would like to be
A professor of
Geometry.

When I grow up
I would like to be
An explorer of
The galaxy.

When I grow up
I would like to be
Given a medal
For bravery.

When I grow up
I would like to be
A miner in a
Colliery.

When I grow up
I would like to be
As big as Dad
Who's six foot three.

When I grow up
I wood like two be
A tipist or a
Sectary.

When I grow up
I would like to be
All sweet and sort
Of sugary.

When I grow up
I would like to be
A pillar of
Society.

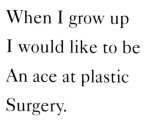

When I grow up
I would like to be
A millionaire
With jewellery.

When I grow up
I would like to be
An ace at plastic
Surgery.

When I grow up
I would like to be
The best there is
At burglary.

When I grow up
I would like to be
Famous for my
Poetry.

When I grow up
I would like to be
A practitioner
Of dentistry.

When I grow up
I would like to be –
ME!

When I grow up
I would like to be
Called "Your Royal
Majesty".

HOMETIME

"Please Miss, these can't be my wellies!
The size and the colour are fine,
My name may be written inside them,
But no way can these ones be mine!"

"Joseph, these must be your wellies!"
"They can't be, I'll prove it," said Joe.
"When I put them down here this morning,
My wellies were covered with snow!"

ROMEO, O ROMEO

"Romeo, O Romeo,
  Wherefore art thou, Romeo?"

    "Here I am, my precious love,
      What aileth thee, my turtle dove?"

"Romeo, O Romeo,
  Of oceans you remind me-O."

    "Why is this, my sweet, fair child,
      Because I'm restless and so wild
        And deep and free, my fluffy chick?"

"No, because you make me sick!"

SIR PERCY BROCKLEHURST POCKETKNIFE

Sir Percy Brocklehurst Pocketknife,

A man who has lived an incredible life,

Has crossed the oceans, sailed the seas,

Traversed the deserts on hands and knees,

Fought his way through mud and slush

To conquer the peaks of the Hindu Kush,

Battled the blizzards to reach the Pole,

Fought Zulus for diamonds in Kimberley's hole,

Lived as a Lama in highest Tibet,

And during the war, let us never forget,

How he saved his battalion from certain doom

By inventing the Brocklehurst legume.

Unfortunately, he has one fatal flaw:

The man is the most astonishing BORE!

He'll tell you tales of daring-do,

But by the time he's half-way through

You're fast asleep, or even worse,

You're still awake! The man's a curse!

His stories are marvellous, first time round,

But after the 96th time, I have found,

After I've listened as long as I can

I just want to get up and strangle the man!

Sir Percy Brocklehurst Pocketknife –

The most boring man I've met in my life.

THE FROGPIG

I'm sad to announce
    That the frogpig's extinct.
We know who's to blame –
    His extinction is linked
To the Frenchman's addiction,
    With knife and with fork,
To frogs' legs and sausages,
    Trotters and pork!

Rana porcus
(Extinct)

THE END

You've had the beginning,
    The bit in the middle,
Now here is the end
    Of my hey diddle diddle.

I hope you enjoyed it,
    It wasn't too boring,
It's just that I thought
    I heard somebody snoring.

My book now is ended,
    No, don't shed a tear;
That's funny, I'm certain
    I heard someone cheer.

So goodbye dear children,
    Enough of this chat,
Did someone just whisper
    "Thank goodness for that?"

THE END

INDEX

Who's Been Sleeping in My Porridge?

COLIN MCNAUGHTON says, "When I was little, I was always
being told to 'stop being silly!' and to 'stop messing about!'. It took me
many years to realize that 'being silly' and 'messing about' are the only things
in life that I'm really good at. Nobody can mess about better than me!
This book is just me doing what I do best."

Colin views his books of verse and pictures as his notebooks. "They're where
I collect my ideas," he says. "Some of these ideas become picture books.
For example, the book *Here Come the Aliens!* (Shortlisted for the
Kate Greenaway Medal) came from the poem 'The Alien Visitor' in *Making
Friends with Frankenstein*, and the book *Have You Seen Who's Just Moved In
Next Door To Us?* (Winner of the Kurt Maschler Award) came from the poem
'There's an Awful Lot of Weirdos in Our Neighbourhood'. As a writer
and illustrator, when I get an idea I think of the words and pictures together:
each poem needs its picture and each picture needs its poem. Neither is
complete without the other." Colin has written three other volumes of verse
and pictures: *There's an Awful Lot of Weirdos in Our Neighbourhood*,
Making Friends with Frankenstein and *Wish You Were Here (And I Wasn't)*
– each of which is also available on cassette, read by Colin himself.

Colin McNaughton's many picture books include *Jolly Roger, Captain Abdul's
Pirate School, Watch Out for the Giant-Killers!, Who's That Banging on the Ceiling?*
and *Dracula's Tomb*, as well as a number of stories about a pig called Preston.
He also illustrated the Red Nose Readers series written by Allan Ahlberg.

ISBN 0-7445-7778-0 (pb)   ISBN 0-7445-7780-2 (pb)   ISBN 0-7445-7755-1 (pb)   ISBN 0-7445-3043-1 (pb)   ISBN 0-7445-4394-0 (pb)